Seven Days with the Gospel of Luke

For a Personal or Shared Retreat

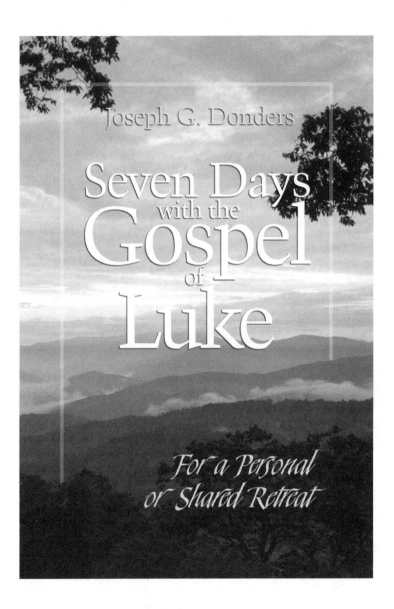

Joseph G. Donders

Seven Days
with the
Gospel
of
Luke

*For a Personal
or Shared Retreat*

TWENTY-THIRD PUBLICATIONS

185 WILLOW STREET • PO BOX 180 • MYSTIC, CT 06355
TEL: 1-800-321-0411 • FAX: 1-800-572-0788
E-MAIL: ttpubs@aol.com • www.23rdpublications.com

Twenty–Third Publications
A Division of Bayard
185 Willow Street
P.O. Box 180
Mystic, CT 06355
(860) 536 - 2611
(800) 321 - 0411
www.twentythirdpublications.com

ISBN:1-58595-387-3
Library of Congress Catalog Card Number: 2004114649
Printed in the U.S.A.

CONTENTS

SUGGESTIONS FOR MAKING A RETREAT

Prepare a quiet place where you can make your retreat. Set up a few symbols that might help create a prayerful atmosphere, such as a statue, a cross, an icon, or a candle. Sit in a comfortable chair. Have a notebook ready to write down your thoughts, feelings, and ideas.

Set a time limit for your reflection; a half-hour to an hour per meditation might do. Use the morning meditation before you begin your day, and the evening meditation either at the end of your work day or before going to bed.

Avoid distractions; try to relax and empty your mind of all worries and concerns. Know that you are in God's presence, that God is present in you, your family, your community, and the world.

Read the Scripture passage cited at the beginning of each meditation. Allow the words to fill your mind. Pause at the words or phrases that speak to you in a particular way, that touch your mind or your heart. Reflect on how the Scripture texts relate to you, your work, your relationships, and your life. The suggestions in the *For Reflection* section will help spark some ideas.

Try to listen to what the Spirit is saying to you. Remember that the most important part of prayer is to be attentive to God's word. Be open to that word, even when it challenges you to live as you have never lived before.

Pray for all those who are making a retreat at the same time as you, and who might even be using this same book. Ask that all of you may be blessed with the knowledge that the Spirit of God is always present, always calling us forward.

Begin a journal that you will use throughout the retreat; there are pages provided for this purpose starting on page 47. Record in it your thoughts and prayers, as well as the moments when you are most aware of God's presence in your life.

INTRODUCTION

Through the pages of this little book, I invite you to reflect on Luke's gospel and use it to make a mini-retreat, a prayerful time away in the midst of your daily tasks and responsibilities. During this seven-day period we will focus together on the spiritual advice found in the gospel of Luke. We will follow the developments—the ups and downs—in the discoveries made by the people who surrounded Jesus.

Every book has its own dynamic, and this is certainly true of the four gospels. Each gospel has its own approach and its own message. Each introduces Jesus in its own way, and is written in response to different needs and different times. Each of the four evangelists tells their story with the desire to help us relate the story to our own lives.

Luke begins his gospel by stating that he knows others have been writing about what happened with Jesus, but that he felt compelled to write his own version. He writes only after careful research, tracing what happened with Jesus from the very beginning of the story. (Luke needed to do this research because he had never met Jesus.)

Luke was not of Jewish stock, but a Gentile. Tradition holds that he was a doctor; we can see this in the way he writes his gospel. Not only does he compare Jesus to a physician (5:31), but he is also more detailed than the other evangelists when he describes the sick people Jesus heals. For example, the other evangelists mention that the mother-in-law of Simon Peter was sick when they visited her at her home in Capernaum; Luke notes that she had a high fever. When the others note that Jesus healed a leper, Luke would add the detail, writing that the man had leprosy all over. He did not mention the disparaging remark about doctors you can find in Mark's gospel, who wrote that a sick woman had suffered greatly at the hands of many doctors (Mk 5:26). Luke had his professional pride!

Luke diagnosed the world in which he lived as a pagan, superstitious world occupied by strangers, that is, the Roman empire. It is obvious from his writings that he did not like what he saw and considered his world dysfunctional and sick. In what we might call a social analysis he related the misery of the masses to the wealth of the few, and identified no less than twenty-four cases of abuse, sin, and corruption in the world of his time.

But then something happened to Luke. On one of his journeys, he found healing spots that give him hope. In Jerusalem he found a community where people lived in common, breaking their bread and sharing their wine, even organizing a food distribution system to help the poor. In Joppa he observed a group of women who, under the guidance of Tabitha and Dorcas, had started what we might call a charity shop to provide clothing for the poor.

When Luke asked the people of these communities why they lived as they did, the answer was always the same: that the Spirit was at work in them, a Spirit they contacted in their prayers, the Spirit of God that had been manifest in Jesus. Luke began to realize that he had fallen among people who lived under immediate divine direction. Wondering about all this Luke tried—and succeeded—in tracing this Spirit to its beginning.

Seven Days with the Gospel of Luke offers suggestions for a morning and evening meditation. The length of that prayerful reflection can differ from person to person and from community to community, but the ideal would be to spend from half an hour to an hour on each session. You can meditate in the quiet of your room, in a church, or even outside—anywhere you feel prayerfully at home with yourself and God's Spirit. There are also suggested questions for your reflection, to help you consider how Luke's gospel applies to your everyday life, as well as a morning and evening prayer you can use to end your meditation. Finally, there is a faith response for each of the seven days.

You can make this retreat alone, with a friend, or with several other people. It can also be adapted to seven weeks, or whatever time period suits your needs.

As we make our retreat, we will reflect on some of the main points in the gospel of Luke. In doing so, we pray that the words of Jesus may affect our lives today as they did the lives of those he touched long ago.

May we come to a new understanding not only of the life of Jesus, but of our own lives as well.

FIRST DAY

MORNING MEDITATION

"To guide our feet into the way of peace"
Read Luke 1:1–80

Luke begins his "orderly account of the events that have been fulfilled among us" with Elizabeth and Zechariah, two people who are not happy with themselves. Elizabeth tells us why; both she and Zechariah have had to endure disgrace from their relatives and neighbors because they are childless. As righteous and pious Jews the two must have been expecting the Messiah, the one who would come to restore the world and to heal the dysfunctional human family. But being barren, they would not be genetically engaged in his coming.

All this radically changes when Gabriel appears to Zechariah during a temple service. The angel told him not to be afraid, and gave him the good news that Elizabeth would conceive and give birth to a son. This son would come to prepare the way for the expected one, the Messiah; he would be "filled with the Holy Spirit." Zechariah had difficulty believing the angel. Because of this, Gabriel told him: "you will become mute, unable to speak, until the day these things occur." And indeed, Elizabeth did conceive.

The story moves fast from this point. When Elizabeth is in her sixth month, Gabriel appears to Mary. We are now no longer in Jerusalem, the center of the Jewish world, but on the periphery, in a small place called Nazareth. Gabriel tells Mary not to be afraid, that she is going to give birth to Jesus, the expected one. Mary asks a question (in Luke's gospel Mary always has questions!): "How can this be, as I am a virgin?" The angel tells her that the Holy Spirit will come upon her, and

3

that her child consequently will be holy, the Son of God. The angel also informs her about what happened to her relative Elizabeth, how she is in her sixth month of pregnancy.

After having heard all the angel had to say, Mary simply replies: "Here I am, the servant of the Lord."

We next read that she is on her way to visit Elizabeth. At the moment the two women meet, they suddenly understand what has happened to them. John leaps for joy in the womb of his mother when meeting Mary and Jesus, and Elizabeth, "filled with the Holy Spirit," is jubilated by Jesus' presence in Mary's womb.

This is the second time Luke uses the phrases "joy" and "filled with the Holy Spirit" in his text. Prior to this, Gabriel uses these words when he announces to Zechariah that a son will be born to him and Elizabeth. The angel tells him that John "would be filled with the Holy Spirit" and that his coming would cause "joy and gladness." Luke uses these expressions over and over again in his gospel. He uses the word "joy" twenty-two times, and the term "filled with the Holy Spirit" eighteen times! God's Spirit breaking into our world could only be a joyful event.

In turn, Elizabeth's joy caused Mary to sing a song of praise, using the words we now know as the Magnificat. Here Mary not only expresses her personal joy at the coming of the Messiah; she also sings of how this will be a blessing for the whole of humanity for all time to come. Her song is one of liberation. Those who rule and terrorize the world will be brought down, and restoration, redemption, and healing will be the order of the day. The whole of the human family will be fed, and the dysfunctionality of the human family will be healed. There will be one table for all, and the promises of old, made to Abraham and Sarah, will be honored. Change is in the air!

Mary and Elizabeth were enthusiastic (a word that means "filled with spirit") about their role in the divine plan. They were willing to cooperate and to render their service to its realization. We too are invited to share in their enthusiasm.

We meet the same Spirit of God in Luke's account of the birth of Elizabeth's child. Zechariah had been living in the silence imposed on him by the angel. But his voice was restored at the naming and circumcision ceremony of his son. The neighbors and relatives wanted to give the child his father's name, Zechariah. Elizabeth protested and told them that his name should be John. No one in the family has ever had that name, they said.

When Zechariah was asked what name he wanted to give his son, he took a writing tablet and wrote: "His name is John." All were amazed by this, but their amazement increased when Zechariah then regained his speech. And he, "filled with the Holy Spirit," began to sing with words that were a prophetic description of the role his son would play. This boy would be a prophet of the Most High, who would prepare the coming of the Lord. He would herald a new dawn for the whole of creation, for all who lived in the darkness of the world. This son would "guide our feet into the way of peace."

At the end of this first chapter Jesus has been in his mother's womb for over three months. Yet a path had already been set out for him. Old promises were at the point of being fulfilled. Expectancy was growing. The people began to understand and believe.

FOR REFLECTION

- Once she understood her role, Mary willingly said, "Yes, let it be!" Are you willing to respond in the same way to God's plans for you?

- How do you feel about our world today? What is your diagnosis? What is your prognosis?

- What can you do to prepare a path for the Lord?

MORNING PRAYER

Greetings, favored one! The Lord is with you. Blessed are you among women, and blessed is the fruit of your womb. Amen.

FAITH RESPONSE FOR TODAY

Let the realization of God's reign of justice and peace overrule the logic of the world in whatever decisions you are asked to make today.

EVENING MEDITATION

"Great joy for all the people"
Read Luke 2:1–52

Without a doubt, Christmas is the best known and most popular feast among Christians—even among many non-Christians!

Luke's account of the birth in a manger, the shepherds who attended Jesus, and the angels who announced his birth is probably the best known Christmas story. Nevertheless, it is a story that has taken on a life of its own, becoming commercialized, overexposed, bland, sentimental, and too familiar. That is why it is good to re-read the original version and ask, what did Luke want to tell?

Everyone knows that Jesus was born in a stable and that Mary laid him in a manger after his birth. You'll find replicas of that stable and crib all over the world in churches, shops, homes, and sometimes even in public places. Almost everyone knows why Jesus was born in such poor surroundings; as Luke's text reads, they "laid him in a manger, because there was no place for them in the inn."

But another interpretation of the text could be this: Mary laid Jesus in a manger because *the inn was no place for him.* In this sense, the fact that he was born outside, practically in the open, is not something to feel badly about. It was something intentional; it *had* to be like that. Jesus' birth in a stable indicates that this birth was a completely new beginning in this world, so new that there was no place for it in the old order, as such. Did not Zechariah speak about the dawn of a new day?

The same kind of newness is also indicated by other details in Luke. He begins his second chapter by referring to the oppressive regime of a Roman emperor, whom he calls by name: Augustus. He then switches from Rome to a backwater region of the empire, and looks at the situation of a poor couple who are in a stable somewhere near Bethlehem.

It is there that the new is born and announced with heavenly fanfare to a group of the most unlikely people: a group of shepherds who are in the fields with their sheep. It is to them that the angels bring the "good news of great joy for all the people," singing "glory to God in the highest heaven and on earth peace."

In their song, the angels promise great joy and peace to all those favored by God. As long as there is human division and discord there can be neither peace nor joy; to put it another way, "It will be one world or no world."

The next person we meet in Luke's story affirms this relationship between "peace" and "all the people." His name is Simeon, and Luke tells us that "the Holy Spirit rested on him." This Spirit drives him to the temple on the day that Joseph and Mary are there to present Jesus. Simeon holds the child in his arms and speaks about peace. He prophesies that Jesus will be a light and salvation for Jews and Gentiles alike. Jesus will be a new beginning for the whole of humanity!

Mary and Joseph are amazed at what they have heard. But Simeon ends his prayer with sobering words: "This child is destined for the falling and the rising of many in Israel, and to be a sign that will be opposed...and a sword will pierce your own soul too." Then Anna, a prophetess, joins the group, praising God and speaking about the child to all those looking forward to redemption. In Luke's gospel, the faith of a man alone never suffices; there is always a woman to confirm it!

Luke's next story tells of the time Jesus was lost in Jerusalem, and found three days later by Mary and Joseph. The three of them had gone to Jerusalem to celebrate the Passover. At the time, Jesus was a boy of twelve. On the way home, his parents realized that they had lost him. Mary must have thought that he was with Joseph, and Joseph that he was with Mary. When the two met after one day of traveling they discovered that Jesus was not with them. They went back to Jerusalem to look for him, but it was only on the third day that they found him in the temple.

This is the third time Luke tells us that both Joseph and Mary were amazed. Mary took her child aside and said to him, "Child, why have you treated us like this? Look, your father and I have been searching for you with great anxiety." Jesus answered her: "Why were you searching for me? Did you not know that I must be in my Father's house?"

Luke notes that neither Mary nor Joseph understood what Jesus was saying. Mary remained wondering, and "treasured all these things in her heart." She seems not to have realized as yet her role as mother of the Messiah. She had yet to learn a lesson we all have to learn: that relating to Jesus means relating to everyone!

Mary had to surrender her child to his role and mission. It was the sword Simeon warned her about. Jesus did not only belong to her family; he belonged to the family of his Father in heaven, the Father of all. Jesus came for all.

FOR REFLECTION

- Globalization is one of the characteristics of our modern world. Where does this process fit in the spirit of the angel's Christmas message?

- How willing are you to act so that peace may be realized for all people? Like Mary, will your heart be pierced because of Jesus?

- In his gospel, Luke puts the birth of Jesus into a political context. Should we do the same? What would be the implications?

EVENING PRAYER

Lord Jesus, help me to walk in peace. Help me to turn the swords in my life into tools of love, understanding, and peace. Amen.

SECOND DAY

MORNING MEDITATION

"Heaven was opened"

Read Luke 3:1–23

In a solemn and detailed way, Luke indicates exactly the time that "the word of God" came to John, making him the Baptizer. We had already learned that John was "filled with the Holy Spirit"; now the Spirit engages him in a dramatic way. Living in the "wilderness" (some Scripture editions translate this as "desert"), he began to prophesy that Isaiah's prediction was going to be fulfilled: "all flesh shall see the salvation of God." The restoration of the world was at hand.

Filled with hope and expectation, people from all over came to listen to him. John told them that the ax was lying at the root of the fruitless old tree, ready to cut it down and burn it in the fire. He told them how the threshing floor of this world would be cleaned up, the grain collected, and the chaff burnt. These are strong and promising metaphors!

John's listeners asked him what they should do. He told them that they should repent their past and—echoing the song Mary prayed when she had come to visit his mother Elizabeth—that those who were rich enough to have two of everything should share with those who had nothing. Further, tax collectors and soldiers should be honest and fair in the exercise of their power.

When some began to think that John himself might be the promised Messiah, he told them he was not the one. He could baptize them with water, symbolically washing away their past. He could even tell them what to do in the present and future. But he could not instill in them the power to accomplish those things. That empowerment was going to be given by someone else, someone who would come after him, someone more powerful than he was—someone who would baptize them with Spirit and fire.

John was like a doctor who, upon meeting a sick patient, could explain that person's illness and know what medicine should be taken, but would not have the means to provide it. It is like a mechanic who knows that a blocked motor needs some lubrication but who does not have the oil to get the thing working.

Eventually, Herod arrested John, but not before John baptized Jesus (though John is not explicitly mentioned as the one who baptizes him). After being baptized, Jesus prays. While he is at prayer heaven opens and the Holy Spirit is seen descending upon him. Jesus, conceived by the power of the Holy Spirit, is now shown as being anointed with that Spirit. Thus, Jesus is the unique bearer of the Spirit of God.

In their accounts of Jesus' baptism, Mark, Matthew, and John all tell us that the Holy Spirit descended upon Jesus as a dove. But Luke is more specific, reporting that the Spirit descended upon him "in *the bodily form* of a dove." He might have done this to avoid the suggestion that it was a form of hallucination or mystical experience. The phrase "bodily form" indicates something tangible, objective, and physical. It is an indication that Spirit and worldly life belong together. The world needs a soul. It has to be changed and transformed under the influence of the Spirit. This bonding of Spirit and life indicates that there is a service to be rendered, a service found within the context of our world.

After the descent of the Spirit, a voice is heard: "You are my Son, the Beloved; with you I am well pleased!" This voice both commends and strengthens Jesus, speaking encouraging words not only for him but also for all those who follow him and share his Spirit.

Heaven had opened when Jesus prayed, and it became clear who he was. The same thing happens when we pray. Heaven opens, telling us who we are and what our task is. Together with Jesus we belong to the same life, the same family: God's family.

Jesus showed his solidarity with the people who had gathered around John the Baptizer, hoping for renewal and healing of their world. He was intent on being engaged in that process, taking on the evil and sinfulness of the world through the power of the Holy Spirit.

In these texts Luke tangibly connects the Holy Spirit and prayer, which reflects his experience upon encountering the early Christian communities. When he asked them why they did the things they did and why they lived according to what he calls, in the Acts of the Apostles, "the Way," they replied that they had been inspired by the Spirit, the Spirit of Jesus. When Luke asked how they had contacted that Spirit, their answer was "in prayer," just as Jesus had promised: "how much more will the heavenly Father give the Holy Spirit to those who ask?" (11:13).

FOR REFLECTION

- How are the events described in this third chapter of Luke's gospel relevant to the world in which we live?
- To what are you called by your own baptism? How far are you willing to go to preach the good news?
- Did you ever refuse to pray when you knew you should have? If so, why? Was there a consequence?

MORNING PRAYER

Come Lord Jesus, help me not be too set in my own ways, but trust in and be faithful to your guidance in my life. Let me be willing to listen to your invitation and your call again and again. Amen.

FAITH RESPONSE FOR TODAY

Reflect on your own baptism. How do you see God's Spirit at work in your life? Take stock of the ways you live out your baptism, and consider whether it is time to do more.

EVENING MEDITATION

"Do not put the Lord your God to the test"
Read Luke 4:1–13

John the Baptizer was living in the wilderness when the Word of God came to him. Jesus, "full of the Holy Spirit," was led into the same wilderness to be tempted by the devil. The temptations Luke describes were not only suffered by Jesus. They are recognizable in the lives of each one of us, as well.

The devil tempts Jesus to use his giftedness only for himself: "If you are the Son of God, command this stone to become a loaf of bread." Jesus refuses, telling his tempter that life is more than bread (or material gain) alone.

Then Satan shows Jesus all the political power in the world, explaining that he is willing to give it all to Jesus if Jesus worships him. Jesus answers that he came to serve only God. There is no desire for material profit or power for him!

In his last challenge the devil puts Jesus on the highest point of the temple, playing out humanity's lust for glory and fame. He taunts Jesus by saying, "If you are the Son of God, throw yourself down from here, for it is written, 'He will command his angels concerning you, to protect you.'" Again, Jesus refuses.

Wealth, power, and fame are the great temptations that turn our world into a jungle. Luke describes them as the perpetual threat to the restoration of the world Jesus came to introduce; that is, the establishment of what Luke calls over forty times in his gospel "the kingdom of God" or "the reign of God."

In addition to using the general terms of wealth, power, and fame to analyze what goes wrong with the world, Luke describes twenty-four specific types of sins and sinners. It is a long list of all kinds of people:

a city-woman who was a sinner (7:37); a heartless priest who left a beat-up traveler bleeding on the road (10:31) and a Levite who did the same (10:32); a lazy man who did not want to help a neighbor (11:7); a hypocritical Pharisee who hid the truth about himself (12:1); a blasphemer who denied the influence of the Holy Spirit (12:10); a successful farmer who thought only of himself (12:19); a legalistic priest who preferred the law to mercy (13:14); a ruler who plotted a violent war (13:31); some people who excused themselves in trivial ways when invited to the Lord's table (14:18); the rebelling and ungrateful prodigal son (15:11); a dishonest accountant (16:1); a rich glutton who did not notice the poor man at his door (16:20); a corruptor of children (17:2); an over-demanding boss (17:8); an unjust judge who refused to help a widow (18:4); a self-righteous Pharisee who showed false piety (18:11); a lazy servant who did not use what was entrusted to him (19:20); some scribes who loved flattery (20:46); ruthless moneylenders who mortgaged and "devoured" the houses of widows (20:47); those who overlooked the coming of God's reign (21:34); the disciples who betrayed Jesus, Judas (22:48) and Peter (22:57); and a politician who thought only of saving his own skin (23:24).

This long catalog of sinners might give the impression that Luke is a pessimist. Indeed, he may have been—until he met people of "the Way," as Christian communities were called in his time. That meeting changed his outlook, although he remained a realist. He looked at his world as a physician would, and diagnosed it as sick. It is in that context that he quotes Jesus calling himself a healer: "Those who are well have no need of a physician, but those who are sick. I have come not call the righteous but sinners to repentance" (5:31–32).

Being a doctor, Luke had an insight into the healing process. When you feel sick and go to a doctor to ask what is wrong with you, the doctor might tell you that you are right; you *are* sick.

When you then ask him or her, "Can you heal me?" a not-too-wise doctor might say, "Yes, I think I can heal you." His or her wise colleague will say: "No, I cannot heal you. You can only heal yourself. Your healing has to come from somewhere within you. What I as a healer can do is stimulate that process with therapy or medication. The power to heal has to come from you."

This is how Luke describes Jesus' healing work among sinners. No one is written off completely. In every person, and consequently in every sinner, there is something divine that can be stimulated. A sinner might be alienated from that divine presence, but it remains there. God is faithful to God's creatures. Jesus came among us, according to Luke, to help the sinner rediscover his or her dignity, notwithstanding all kinds of hurts and wounds.

It is here that we find the difference between John the Baptizer and Jesus himself. John condemned sin, as did Jesus. But John remained dressed in his austere and penitential garment as a signal that the old would soon pass away, and the new was going to come.

The new came in Jesus. By his own life he demonstrated what the new life, the reign of God, was about. He lived it, and living it, it began to attract others, awakening God's breath in them and allowing them to joyfully discover their own true selves.

FOR REFLECTION

- The Spirit of Christ motivated the lives of those in the early Christian communities. How is the Spirit of Christ alive in your own life today? What are its signs?

- Which of the three is the greatest temptation in your life: wealth, power, or fame? How do you resist this temptation?

- As you read the newspaper, look at the evening news, or listen to a radio news broadcast over the next few days, be aware of how the three temptations Jesus overcame in the desert still terrorize our world today.

EVENING PRAYER

Loving God, lead me not into temptation, and deliver me from all evil.
For yours is the kingdom, the power and the glory. Amen.

THIRD DAY

"To proclaim the year of the Lord's favor"

Read Luke 4:14–30

Having tested Jesus, the devil (some people would prefer to say '"the evil power in this world") "departed from him until an opportune time." The devil was not going to give up on Jesus; he would wait for another chance. In this way Luke sets the scene for the whole of Christ's ministry, as well as for the life of the Church and its ministry, and even for our own lives: led by the Spirit; tempted by the devil.

The old world Jesus came to restore and heal was not and is not going to give up without a lot of resistance! Luke illustrates this in great detail when he describes how Jesus introduces himself to his own community in Nazareth. When he arrives in Nazareth—the place, Luke adds, where he grew up and was accustomed to go to the synagogue each Sabbath—his fame had already spread throughout the countryside. That is why the synagogue must have been full that Sabbath.

The people expected Jesus to do the reading from the Torah, and he complied. As he stood up to read, the scroll of the prophet Isaiah was given to him. (Luke does not mention whether Jesus had asked for that part of Scripture, or whether they just gave it to him.) Once he received the scroll, Jesus rolled it down to the passage he wanted to read to the people, and declared:

"The Spirit of the Lord is upon me,
  because he has anointed me
  to bring good news to the poor.

He has sent me to proclaim release to the captives,
    and recovery of sight to the blind,
    to let the oppressed go free,
    to proclaim the year of the Lord's favor."

Jesus then rolled up the scroll, gave it back to the attendant, and sat down. This was an indication that he was going to teach. Luke describes the tension of that moment: "The eyes of all in the synagogue were fixed on him." Jesus had just read one of the clearest prophecies announcing the coming of the Messiah and the new order he was going to introduce "the year of the Lord's favor," the year of the Jubilee!

Jesus then began to speak; you could hear a pin drop. He said: "Today this scripture has been fulfilled in your hearing," using Isaiah's quote to introduce his ministry. The people were amazed by his words and wondered, "Is not this Joseph's son?" Didn't they know him and his family? Hadn't Jesus grown up among them? He asked them to not think about him in that way any more but as the prophet promised by Isaiah. He pointed out that a prophet always had difficulties being recognized in his own hometown.

Jesus then alluded to the fact that he knew they had heard about the miracles he had been working in Capernaum, and that they had been complaining. Why had he not done those things in Nazareth? Was that not the place he came from and belonged to? He then went one step further, infuriating them. Jesus made it very clear that, being filled with the Holy Spirit, his prophetic role was not limited to them, to his own people. His work included the whole of the human family.

Jesus reminded the people of two stories that they knew well, one about a woman and one about a man. The first story was about a non-Jewish woman at Zarephath, who was helped by God through the prophet Elijah at a time when the Jewish widows were in great need. The second story was about a Syrian army commander, Naaman, who was healed of leprosy by God through the prophet Elisha, when many Jewish men who were suffering from the same disease were not healed.

Hearing those stories, the people realized what Jesus wanted to tell them: the restoration of the world was not only going to be for them. It was going to be for all. The whole of the dysfunctional human family was going to be healed.

This was too much for the people of Nazareth. Jumping up they chased Jesus out of the synagogue, out of the town, up to the brow of the hill, intending to throw him down and to kill him. Facing them, Jesus escaped and "went on his way."

The people of Nazareth wanted Jesus for themselves alone. They were exclusive, thinking only of themselves. It is a trap and a temptation that is still with us today.

FOR REFLECTION

- Have you ever acted in a "prophetic" manner when confronting an unjust situation? What was the outcome?

- In your opinion, why is it that "no prophet is accepted in the prophet's hometown"? How does this affect any decision you may make to act in a prophetic manner?

- What is your feeling about the treatment of refugees and so-called illegal immigrants in your country? Is the passage that we reflected on this morning of any relevance to you in this regard?

MORNING PRAYER

Jesus Christ, you ask us to do good and help others in your universal spirit of love. Forgive us for preferring to serve ourselves.
Lord have mercy! Amen.

FAITH RESPONSE FOR TODAY

Recall a contemporary person who, in his or her search for just and equitable treatment for all, was persecuted and perhaps even killed because of their prophetic stance. Read a book or article on this person; if you have access to the Internet you can use this to obtain some information about him or her.

EVENING MEDITATION

"He spoke with authority"
Read Luke 4:31—5:32

Jesus chased away evil spirits, healed sick and disabled people, multiplied bread and fish, calmed storms and seas, forgave sins, and brought dead people to life; but he also did something else. Jesus stirred something in people. They felt uplifted simply by being in his company. He awakened and enlivened the spirit within them. That is why it was said that he spoke with authority.

The word "authority" comes from a Latin root that means "making something grow." *That* is what happened to people in Jesus' company. Jesus made feel them great, discovering in themselves dimensions they had never discovered before. George Bernard Shaw once wrote that the great person is the one who makes others realize that they are great. G.K. Chesterton added that this is why Jesus is the greatest of all.

This authority must have been one of the reasons that in Luke's gospel the crowds around Jesus kept growing as he moved from town to town (8:4). Everywhere he went the crowds were waiting for him and welcomed him, eventually growing so large "that they trampled on one another" (12:1). Jesus, himself "filled with the Holy Spirit," brought forth this same Spirit in them.

Jesus asks more than ninety questions in Luke's gospel. At least seventy of these questions are intended to evoke answers. Jesus wanted the crowds around him—and us, as well—to discover their inner light. Twice he invited the people to let their light shine, not to hide it under a jar or under a bed, but to put it on a lampstand so that all might benefit from the light (8:16; 11:33). Jesus came to unearth God's presence in us, to release the divine spirit blown into us from the very beginning. He came to remind us of our dignity.

The first miracle that Luke describes in some detail is when Jesus "rebuked" an evil spirit that had taken over a man who was with Jesus in the synagogue of Capernaum. It is a simple story, but a grandiose sign of what was going to happen in our world.

A local fisherman, Simon, invited Jesus to his house. There they told Jesus that Simon's mother-in-law was sick. (Luke, the physician, tells us that she had a high fever.) Jesus went to her, bent graciously over her, and "rebuked" her fever. It is interesting to note that Luke uses the same word as he did when Jesus chased away the evil spirit from the man in the synagogue. The woman, whose name is not mentioned, gets up and immediately follows the example of service and kindness that Jesus had showed her. Not only is she saved, but the Spirit calls her immediately to serve! This call and response is also found in the following story.

Simon, who is now called Simon Peter, lends his boat to Jesus so he can address the crowd from the lake. After Jesus had finished speaking, he told Simon where to put in his net. Doing so, he catches an enormous amount of fish. At this, he falls on his knees at Jesus' feet, saying: "Go away from me, Lord, for I am a sinful man!"

At that moment, Simon describes and defines himself as worthless, not called to anything worthwhile. Jesus does not agree. He tells him, as well as Peter's partners James and John, who were witnessing the scene, "Do not be afraid, from now on you will be catching people." The three left everything and followed Jesus, spreading the good news as they healed and changed the world.

When Luke tells the story of Levi, the tax collector, he is even more brief. Jesus simply says to him, "Follow me." And so he did, moved from within by Jesus. Afterward, Levi threw a "great banquet" for his colleagues and friends, including Jesus and his disciples. Here Jesus is questioned by the Pharisees: "Why do you eat and drink with tax collectors and sinners?" And Jesus replies, "I have come to call not the righteous but sinners to repentance."

Throughout this passage the authority of Jesus is questioned. Luke continues these questions in the Acts of the Apostles, indicating that the question of Jesus' authority is at issue in our lives, as well.

Think of people like Archbishop Oscar Romero or Mother Teresa of Calcutta. Where did their inspiration, their motivation come from?

Why did they do what they did? Think of yourself: where did you find the motivation to make this retreat? What inspires you to live a more saintly life, to fulfill your duties as well as possible? What about the thousands and thousands of Christian organizations whose members invest their goodwill in voluntary work, renewal programs, and monetary donations: from where does their authority come?

The answer is simply this: from the Spirit of God, whom they and we recognize in Jesus Christ. It is the Spirit of Jesus active in us. All graciousness and kindness, love and respect come from that affiliation. Christ is born again and again through the good works and faith of those who are faithful to that relationship.

FOR REFLECTION

- Did you ever withdraw from doing something of service for someone because you did not think yourself holy enough? Reflect on how all are called by baptism to continue the healing service of Jesus in our world.

- Have you ever said," I am only a human being!" thus denying all that you are and are intended to be?

- Where and how have you seen someone stirred by the Spirit of Jesus? What did you notice?

EVENING PRAYER

Jesus Christ, you have told us to be the light of the world. Help me to live as your light, notwithstanding the difficulties it might cause. Amen.

FOURTH DAY

MORNING MEDITATION

"Blessed are you…"

Read Luke 6:12–36

After a night of prayer on a mountaintop Jesus calls his disciples up to join him. He then chooses twelve of them, and names them "apostles." With the twelve and the rest of his disciples Jesus descends to meet the crowds waiting for him at the bottom of the mountain. He then starts to teach them about how to relate to God and to each other in the new reign of God.

In the gospel of Matthew, Jesus gives this instruction from the height of a mountain, and it is known as the Sermon on the Mount. Luke situates this instruction on a "level place" in the plain, using it as a metaphor for the world in which we live.

Jesus begins this teaching with a set of blessings and ends with a set of woes, echoing the words of his mother Mary when she met Elizabeth:

"Blessed are you who are poor, hungry, weeping…"

"But woe to you who are rich, filled, laughing…."

These words sound harsh to some ears, and hopeful to the ears of others. A reversal is going to take place at the beginning of the reign of God. Jesus offers his congratulations and best wishes to those who are poor, hungry, and weeping. Their situation is going to be changed and reversed. Jesus also addresses those who are rich, overfed, and laughing, smug in their state of affairs; this will change, as well.

A new balance will be struck. The prayer Jesus later on will teach both groups to pray is going to be heard:

"Father, hallowed be your name. Your kingdom come. Give us each day our daily bread" (11:2–3).

Jesus adds one last "blessing" and "woe." He blesses and congratulates those who are willing to engage themselves in the new world to come, though they will be persecuted because of it. He tells them not to lose courage, to leap for joy because their persecution shows that they are on the right path, his Way. He warns those who are praised, who do not suffer any difficulty or contradiction, because they are not engaged in the new world that is to come.

Jesus foresees that the old will not bend to the new without resistance. In fact the scribes and Pharisees, the leaders of the existing order, had already been coming together to discuss "what they might do to Jesus" (6:11). They did not want him to heal the sick on the Sabbath day. They preferred their law to his compassion and humanity.

Reading the beatitudes and the woes that follow might give the impression that Jesus condemns the rich for their wealth. In Luke's gospel, however, Jesus never condemns wealth as such. He had many rich friends, and he loved to wine and dine with them (7:36; 11:37; 14:1,7). In fact, Jesus was even blamed for this by some, who called him a glutton and a drunkard, a friend of tax collectors and sinners (7:34).

Jesus accepted the support of the wealthy. Joanna and Susanna provided for him and his disciples out of their resources (8:3); after his death he was buried by a rich and influential acquaintance, Joseph of Arimathea, a man who was "waiting expectantly for the kingdom of God" (23:51).

Wealth itself is not the problem, but its power and the way it is used. Luke recounts no less than eighteen times how Jesus warns of the dangers of being rich. It can be a serious hurdle to entering the reign of God: "How hard it is for those who have wealth to enter the reign of God! For it is easier for a camel to pass through the eye of a needle than for a rich person to enter the reign of God" (18:24–25).

In the story about the rich man and Lazarus (16:19–31), Jesus does not blame the man for eating and drinking his fill but for completely overlooking Lazarus, who daily sat outside his door. In another parable, a rich landowner is called a "fool" because he thinks only of himself, building new barns to store his wealth.

Likewise, Jesus did not praise the poor for their poverty. The poor could also be greedy, envious, and so taken up by their daily worries that they had no time for anything else.

The story of Zacchaeus stands as an example of what should happen (19:2–10). This tax collector, addicted to money, changes when he is touched by Jesus. He decides to repay fourfold the people whom he had defrauded and to share a considerable amount of what was left over with the poor.

The beatitudes teach that it is the duty of everyone who is gifted in a special way—whether time, talent, or treasure—to share, to do good, to give, to feed the hungry, to dress the naked, and to be hospitable to the homeless. As Jesus himself once said, "It is more blessed to give than to receive" (Acts 20:35).

FOR REFLECTION

- Where do you fit in the categories Jesus mentions in his teaching on the plain: among those blessed or those warned?

- Have you ever been excluded, defamed, or reviled on account of Jesus and the reign of God he came to introduce? What form did this persecution take?

- Does your being a disciple of Jesus have an influence on your political preferences and decisions? Why or why not?

MORNING PRAYER

Come, Jesus, and help me understand that doing something good for someone is to say "Yes" to the will of the Father. Amen.

FAITH RESPONSE FOR TODAY

Look carefully through the unsolicited mail that asks for your help this week. Choose one, and consider sending a donation or volunteering your time and talent.

EVENING MEDITATION

"Lord, teach us to pray"

Read Luke 11:1–13; 18:1–14

As Luke visited different kinds of Christian communities, he met women and men who lived under direct divine guidance. When making decisions in life, these people simply said: "For it has seemed good to the Holy Spirit and to us that…" (Acts 15:28). When Luke asked how they came to know God's Spirit, the Spirit of Jesus, they replied that it was through prayer.

Prayer was the key to understanding the sometimes extraordinary behavior of the members of these early Christian communities. The more he spoke with these people, the more Luke became convinced that prayer was also the key to understanding Jesus and empathizing with his life and his mission.

For Luke, Jesus is a person of prayer. It is prayer that guides his life. It is while at prayer that he makes his decisions. He prays at his baptism, when tempted in the desert, when choosing the twelve, at his transfiguration, in the garden at the Mount of Olives before his arrest, and on the cross.

Again and again Luke tells us how Jesus went off into the mountains to be with his Father in prayer. He teaches his disciples how to pray with the words "Our Father…." He gives them parables on how to pray and invites them to pray always. He specifically tells them to ask for the Holy Spirit.

It is that last invitation, or might we say requirement, that makes prayer so difficult, so risky. John the Baptizer once said that his successor, Jesus, would baptize the people with Spirit and fire. Asking for the Holy Spirit, inviting that kind of contact with God, means playing with that fire!

In prayer we come to know who we are, come in contact with ourselves and realize what is asked of us. This is what happened to Jesus when he prayed: "Father, if you are willing, remove this cup from me: yet not my will but yours be done!" (22:42). He knew what the consequence of his prayer would be.

When we pray, "Give us each day our daily bread," do we ever think about the millions and millions of starving people in our world? If we restrict that "us" to only ourselves, don't we escape the consequence of that prayer?

In his four parables on prayer Jesus teaches us not so much *what* to pray for, but *how* to pray. In the first one, which he relates immediately after teaching the Our Father, he speaks about a man who, in need of something to eat for an unexpected guest, goes to a friend to ask for help. This parable suggests that we should approach God as our friend. We should also approach Jesus in this way, as he called us "my friends" (12:4). In the second parable Jesus compares those who we address in our prayers to a parent who is good to his or her children, giving them what they ask for (11:9–13).

While those two parables tells us about the love of God we experience in our prayer, in chapter 18 Jesus tackles two other prayer issues. The first story (18:1–8) is about a widow who asks an unjust and unfair judge to do her justice. The man has "no fear of God, and no respect for anyone." He refuses to help her. But the widow does not give up, even threatening the judge physically, and the man gives in "quickly."

In this intriguing story the unjust judge does *not* stand in for God. The story is about the widow and her perseverance. She is presented as a model for situations where justice should be done and injustice amended. It is our insistence and our repeated prayer that will help us be faithful to God's will and work at what should be done, inspired by God's Spirit.

The last parable (18:9–14) is about a Pharisee and a tax collector. Both went up to the temple to pray, with one standing in front of the temple and the other in the back. In the original Greek, Luke tells that the Pharisee was "praying to himself." He exalted himself, and looked down on those who were not as "pious" and "law-abiding" as he thought himself to be. He obviously belonged to that group of people of whom Jesus said: "Woe to you who are laughing now!"

In the back of the temple the tax collector, bending down and not daring to look up at heaven, was beating his breast, saying: "God be merciful to me, a sinner!" He belonged to the people of whom Jesus had said: "Blessed are you who are weeping now!" Finishing his story Jesus confirmed this reversal, when he said: "This man went down to his home justified rather than the other; for all who exalt themselves will be humbled, but all who humble themselves will be exalted."

FOR REFLECTION

- How does your life in its different aspects—married or single, working or retired, healthy or ailing—contribute to the realization of the reign of God?

- Where in our world is the absence of prayer most felt? In what situations is its presence best experienced?

- Reflect on the influence of prayer in your life. When you have a chance, talk with someone about his or her experience of prayer, sharing your own thoughts and experience.

EVENING PRAYER

Lord Jesus, teach me how to pray! Give me the courage
to assess my life in all humility. Amen.

FIFTH DAY

Lost and found

Read Luke 15:1–32

Luke is the only evangelist who gives us the parable of the prodigal son, his father, and his older brother. It is often seen as the heart of his gospel, and it is definitely one of the best-loved of Jesus' parables.

Luke introduces the parable with two other stories. The first parable is that of the good shepherd, who seems to be more interested in the one sheep he lost than in the ninety-nine others that dependably followed him. In the second story, also a parable that only Luke records, Jesus speaks of a woman who had ten silver coins, but having lost one lights a lamp and sweeps her house carefully until she finds it. Then, in her enthusiasm, she invites neighbors and friends to celebrate with her.

These parables can be interpreted in different ways. (One of the advantages and strengths of parables is that they are open to different interpretations.) You can explain the behavior of the shepherd who lost one sheep by highlighting his love for the stray one. You can also explain it by pointing out that, having lost one sheep, the totality of his flock was flawed. One hundred is a nice round number; ninety-nine is not.

Gregory of Nyssa, an ancient Christian wisdom figure, applied the second interpretation to the story of the woman who lost one coin. As long as she had ten coins, things were complete. Applying this to the inner life of the woman herself, Gregory said the woman was a "whole" person. The ten coins stood for the woman herself. Having lost one coin meant that she lost herself. Finding it she found herself. Gregory even suggested that the lost coin stood for Jesus Christ.

The two stories introduce the main one, the story of the prodigal son. In his encyclical on God the Father, which he gave the title "Rich in Mercy," Pope John Paul II gave a beautiful interpretation of that main story.

The younger son, the prodigal one, acts in a heartless way. He practically tells his father, "Get lost, I am not interested in you, I am only interested in the money that will be my share once you are dead." His father, who must have been heartbroken, gives him the money, and the son leaves the next day. As time goes on, he squanders his money and ends up working in a pig sty, which was a shocking horror for a Jew. Being hungry and not even allowed to share the pig fodder, he "came to himself." And here the story begins to resemble Gregory of Nyssa's interpretation of the lost coin story.

After having wasted his father's money, the prodigal son realizes that he may have also wasted his own life up to this point. He thinks he can no longer consider himself as the son of his father. In desperation, not knowing what else to do, he decides to go his father and ask, since he knew he could no longer be considered his son, could the father take him on as a servant?

So the son went to the place that once was his home. While he was still far off, his father saw him coming. Filled with compassion, he ran to meet his son, hugged him and kissed him, and would not even allow his son to finish his speech about his revoked sonship. Looking at his blistered bare feet, his father called for sandals, the best robe, and a ring. At the same time he gave the order to organize an extravagant welcome home party. To him his son had never really been lost; he had remained his son. It is like that maverick sheep who was sought by the good shepherd until it was found, and the coin that could not remain lost as long as the woman frantically looked for it.

The prodigal son had never been completely lost to the heart of his father, and consequently, neither was he lost to his own heart. Thomas Merton, the well-known Trappist monk, once wrote that at the center of all of us there is something "which is untouched by sin and illusion, a point of pure truth, a point or spark that belongs entirely to God, the pure glory of God" (*Conjectures of a Guilty Bystander*).

This reality might seem lost to us at times, but that does not mean it has gone away. It is God's contact point in us, like an ever-growing

Candle-Light

Day has its sun,
And night the stars,
But God has candle-light.

Upon the world's great candle-stick He sets
The little taper of yourself ashine,
That when the sun has sputtered out
And all the stars are dead,
Your immorality may flame and burn
Across His infinite immensity forever.

Wherefore He will sometime blow out the sun,
And snuff the stars,
Preferring candle-light.

Sister Madeleva, CSC

spark, although at times it might be hidden under the ashes of our "prodigal" life. In Luke's gospel, this spark of fire starts to glow and rekindle in all kinds of persons, both sinners and saints, in the presence of Jesus Christ!

After all the initial rejoicing, the older son of the father enters the parable. He is angry that his younger brother is welcomed back as he is. He protests, and facing his father says, "Listen! For all these years I have been working like a slave for you, and I have never disobeyed your command; yet you have never given me even a young goat so that I might celebrate with my friends."

His father appeases him, saying: "Child, you are always with me and all that is mine is yours. But we have to celebrate and rejoice because this brother of yours was lost (to me and to himself) and now he is found (by me and by himself)."

FOR REFLECTION

- With which of the two brothers do you most empathize, the younger one or the older one? Why?

- Are you willing to apply the lesson of the story of the prodigal son—that everyone is loved by God—to everyone around you?

- When have you experienced the power of forgiveness in your life, either by forgiving or by being forgiven? Do you really mean it when you pray, "Father, forgive me, as I forgive others"?

MORNING PRAYER

Dear Jesus, Good Shepherd, help us come together as one, united in justice and peace for the well being of all the world. Amen.

FAITH RESPONSE FOR TODAY

Offer forgiveness today. This can be to someone in your life who has wronged you in some way; or it can be more general, to a person or group whose actions have caused ill for you or your community.

EVENING MEDITATION

"The better part"

Read Luke 7:11–15; 8:40–56; 10:38–42; 13:11–13

Many of the stories that are found only in the gospel of Luke are about women. Luke pays more attention to women than do the other evangelists. He is the one who tells how Jesus took pity on the widow at Nain as she walked behind the bier of her only son. Jesus stopped that funeral procession and gave her son back to her, alive.

Another exclusively unique Lukan story is about the bent-over woman. According to the understanding of those days her disablement was due to an evil spirit. The text even reads that she was someone whom "Satan bound for eighteen long years." In a more contemporary interpretation she represents the situation of women in her day, which continues for many women even in our day. It was, and indeed is, an evil spirit that keeps women oppressed and bent-over.

With only a few words, Luke describes the incident in a striking way. Jesus was teaching in a synagogue on the Sabbath when he noticed the woman. She must have been standing apart from the men, together with the women, as was the temple rule. It was quite significant not only that Jesus saw her but that he even paid attention to her. He interrupted his teaching and called her over. All the eyes in the synagogue must have been fixed on her as she approached Jesus, just as it was at the beginning of his ministry in Nazareth.

Jesus simply said, "Woman, you are set free" as he laid his hands on her. Both of these actions—addressing the woman and touching her—were practically out of the question in that day and age. Was she not considered to be with an evil spirit and therefore unclean?

"Immediately," the woman stood up straight, and under the influence of the Spirit flowing from Jesus' hands she began to praise God.

The leader of the synagogue, who did not dare challenge Jesus directly, protested to the crowd: healings should not be worked on the Sabbath, he said. Jesus called him a hypocrite, and the woman "a daughter of Abraham," restoring and confirming her dignity and place in society. The crowd responded enthusiastically.

Another story exclusive to Luke is the account of Jesus' visit to Martha and Mary. Here there is no mention of their brother Lazarus. After welcoming Jesus, Martha disappears into the kitchen to prepare him a meal, while Mary "sat at the Lord's feet and listened to what he was saying." Jesus is teaching Mary as he did his twelve apostles!

But Martha comes out to protest, asking Jesus to send Mary into the kitchen to help her. Jesus does not do what Martha asked him to do, telling her that Mary had chosen "the better part."

Spiritual authors and commentators throughout the centuries have tried to interpret what happened that day. Is it possible that, at that moment, Jesus did for Mary what he had done for the bent-over woman in the synagogue; that is, showing her he took her as seriously as he did Simon Peter and the others, thus freeing her from a position into which she, as a woman, had been put by the culture of the time? This attitude was unheard of in those days—as it still is today, in many cultures and in many ways.

We can also consider this: by her question, did Martha show an eagerness as well to be unbound from her cultural role, and to share with her sister "the better part"?

Jesus started a process in this world. He did not leave us in a freeze-frame, set in time forever and ever. Jesus himself compared the kingdom of God to the "yeast that a woman took and mixed in with three measures of flour (he knew the recipe!) until all of it was leavened"(13:20–21). He compared the coming of the reign of God to a mustard seed planted in a garden and growing into a mighty tree (13:18–19). He compared it to seed falling on rich soil, adding that it would bear fruit "through perseverance" (8:15), which is an essential virtue in any ongoing process. He asked his disciples to look at the buds slowly unfolding and opening up on a fig tree, to understand what was, and is, happening in our world (21:29–30).

Jesus did not leave us with a fixed world. In fact, he came to deliver us from that kind of world. He came to empower us with the Holy Spirit, *his*

Spirit, a Spirit given not only as a personal, spiritual blessing but also as a responsibility and a mission.

According to Luke, women play an important role in this mission. Women are the first ones to hail the incarnation of Jesus. They accompany him during his public ministry and provide for him from their personal resources. They are the last to leave the cross and the first to announce his resurrection. In all these instances, they have chosen the better part.

FOR REFLECTION

- Do you ever find yourself in a situation where you defend the old because you are afraid of the demands of the new or because you judge that the price to pay for the new is too high for you?

- Have you ever had the experience of being unbound and freed from an illness, difficulty, addiction, or obsession?

- What are the developments in your world that show the budding (and flourishing) of the coming reign of God? Take some time to consider this question.

EVENING PRAYER

Dear Lord, when this world seems to be without hope,
come and inspire me with your life. Help me inspire others
so that your life may flourish within them, as well. Amen.

SIXTH DAY

"The Lord appointed seventy others"
Read Luke 9:1–6; 10:1–24

Luke was not a Jew but what even today Jews call a Gentile. Yet Luke's gospel shows that he was very knowledgeable about Judaism, its Scripture, and its customs. He knew that Jesus could only be understood and appreciated in a Hebrew context. However, he was also convinced that Jesus came for the whole of humanity. He had seen for himself how God's Spirit, the Spirit of Jesus, was manifest and at work in people of all races, cultures, and nationalities.

From the very beginning of his gospel Luke explains that Jesus had the whole world in his view. He does not trace Jesus' genealogy back only to Abraham (and Sarah) as Matthew did in his family tree (1:1–2), but to Adam (and Eve), the ancestors of all humankind. Luke stresses this same universality in the Acts of the Apostles, when writing about Jesus' ascension into heaven. When the disciples ask him, "Lord, is this the time that you will restore the kingdom to Israel?" he answers by sending them "to the ends of the earth" (Acts 1:6–8).

His contemporaries often misunderstood Jesus' universal approach. Remember what happened when he implied in Nazareth that he had come to realize "the year of the Lord's favor" not only for them, but also for those whom they considered "outsiders," mentioning the Gentile widow at Zarephath and the pagan army commander Naaman? The Nazareans wanted to throw Jesus off a cliff!

There were other occasions when the people around Jesus had difficulties with his global approach; for example, when he welcomed sinners like Zacchaeus (19:1–10), the "sinful woman" in Simon's house (7:36–50), Samaritans, lepers, the homeless, and disabled people. When his own disciples sternly forbade mothers to bring their children to him, Jesus reprimanded them, saying: "Let the little children come to me, for it is unto these that the kingdom of God belongs" (18:15–16). It would have been interesting to have seen the faces of the twelve at that moment!

While Mark and Matthew tell how Jesus sent his twelve apostles out on a mission to heal, tackle evil spirits, and to announce the coming of the reign of God, Luke adds the story of a similar mission to "seventy others."

Sometimes the use of a particular number in Scripture is easy to figure out: the number twelve, for example, might refer to the twelve tribes of Israel. But what about that number seventy? The first time a total of seventy is mentioned in Hebrew Scripture is in chapter 10 of Genesis. The chapter, often titled "The Dispersal of the Nations," lists the names of the seventy (in some versions, seventy-two) grandsons born to Noah after the flood. It tells how they left their grandparents' homestead, and, in spreading out all over the world, become the origin of all the different nations and cultures on earth.

We do not need to go overseas to join the mission of the "seventy others" in announcing the kingdom of God. We can be part of that mission while staying on our own street, in our own neighborhood. We can all be involved in that mission cross-culturally and inter-religiously, as well.

Pope John Paul II insists again and again on the need for all Christians to be all involved in this process. In his letter written for the new millennium that began in the year 2000, he wrote:

> It is in this context also that we should consider the great challenge of inter-religious dialogue to which we shall still be committed in the new millennium, in fidelity to the teachings of the Second Vatican Council.... In the years of preparation for the Great Jubilee the Church has sought to build, not least through a series of highly symbolic meetings, a relationship of openness and dialogue with the followers of other religions. This dialogue must continue. In the climate of increased cultural and religious pluralism which

is expected to mark the society of the new millennium, it is obvious that this dialogue will be especially important in establishing a sure basis for peace and warding off the dread specter of those wars of religion which have so often bloodied human history. The name of the one God must become increasingly what it is: a name of peace and a summons to peace. (*Novo Millennio Ineunte*)

FOR REFLECTION

- The Vatican document *Dialogue and Proclamation* indicates that we can become involved in the mission to "gather into one the dispersed children of God" (John 11:52) by engaging in:

  1. *The dialogue of life*, just by being a good neighbor, sharing our joys and sorrows;

  2. *The dialogue of action*, working together to deal with existing social justice issues in our neighborhood and in the world;

  3. *The dialogue of religious experience*, sharing our spiritual riches in prayer and action.

  Where in your daily life do you see ways that these three "dialogues" can begin or continue?

- How might you understand your baptismal mission in a more global perspective?

MORNING PRAYER

Dear Lord Jesus, help me to grow more aware of your life-giving presence throughout our world, according to your Spirit present in me. Amen.

FAITH RESPONSE FOR TODAY

Introduce yourself to a "stranger" in your neighborhood, parish, or at work, in the spirit of the suggestions made above.

EVENING MEDITATION

The Way

Read Luke 9:51–62; 22:7–30

In everyone's life there comes a definitive moment when a decision must be made about which direction to take in life. Luke describes that decisive moment in the life of Jesus: "When the days drew near for him to be taken up, he set his face to go to Jerusalem."

Jesus had been journeying before. In fact, from the moment of his baptism he had been on the road, going from place to place. But now he would take a definite and final direction. He did not travel alone; he never did. He was always accompanied by his apostles, as well as by the women who traveled with him. Luke explicitly names them: Mary from Magdala, Joanna, Susanna, and "many others" (8:1–3). These women would follow him to his death on the cross.

This journey continued for the men and women who followed Jesus. After his death and resurrection, they even called themselves the people of "the Way." We find that self-chosen name mentioned eight times in Luke's other book, the Acts of the Apostles. The name "Christians" was given to the followers of Jesus much later, by others in Antioch (Acts 11:26).

From the moment of his decision up to his initially triumphant arrival in Jerusalem (19:28–46), Jesus is accompanied not only by his followers but by all kinds of other people. He often has a meal with them; no other evangelist places Jesus at as many meals as Luke, who describes at least nine of them, sometimes in great detail.

One of these meals is the evening picnic Jesus organized for a crowd of thousands—the men alone numbered about 5,000. His disciples had wanted to send everyone away to take care of themselves, but he told them: "You give them something to eat" (9:13). Welcoming the whole crowd, Jesus asked them to sit down, and he helped his disciples feed all of them.

Jesus loved meals! It was during a meal that he showed God's mercy when a woman came to anoint his feet. During a meal he promised to be with us always. We usually call that meal the "last supper," but that is really a misnomer. Jesus explicitly asks his disciples to keep organizing such meals "in remembrance of me," assuring us at the same time of his lasting companionship.

Sometimes, following Jesus is not an easy task. As he traveled to Jerusalem, Jesus was on his way to the cross. He knew what it would cost to bring the reign of God to a world bedeviled by sin. When a man came to him at the beginning of his journey to Jerusalem, saying, "I will follow you wherever you go," Jesus warned him, "the Son of Man has nowhere to lay his head." To another one who first wanted to bury his father before following him, he said: "Let the dead bury their own dead"; in other words, forget about taking care of the past. To a third one, who wanted to bid his family farewell, Jesus responded, "No one who puts a hand to the plow and looks back is fit for the kingdom of God."

These are radical but realistic sayings that indicate what it means to follow Jesus on his way. Before he left for Jerusalem he told the disciples what awaited him there. The old, corrupt order was not going to welcome him. It would try to finish him off once and for all. Jesus then added: "If anyone want to become my followers, let them deny themselves and take up their cross daily and follow me" (9:22–23). He repeated this advice and warning once more on his way to Jerusalem: "Whoever does not carry the cross and follow me cannot be my disciple" (14:27).

These words do not mean that we should indulge in life-debasing mortifications. They intend to explain that we should say "no" to all that tempts us not to walk with Jesus, not to take up his cross. Our cross involves both saying "no" to temptation while saying "yes" to accompanying Jesus "into the way of peace" (1:79).

In speaking about this mission, Jesus adds the word "daily." Following him is not only a lofty ideal; it has to do with our daily life, our decisions, tribulations, and conflicts as well as justice, peace, and care for the whole of creation.

Walking the Way of Jesus is an ongoing affair. In those who walk and live it, the reign of God has come among us. To follow his Way is a decision that will color our lives in each waking moment. It is the only way to our true selves and to the fullness of life.

FOR REFLECTION

- When you participate in the Eucharist, are you fully aware that you, together with those present, are sharing a meal with Jesus and with each other? What are, or what should be, the consequences of this table fellowship?

- Recall a person who follows Jesus' Way in an exemplary manner, whether a saint, a noted person in our time, or someone you know from your everyday life. What characteristics, qualities, or deeds prompted you to choose this person?

- Who among your own family members, co-workers, or friends is walking the Way although it may cause them difficulty? Are you walking that Way?

EVENING PRAYER

Dear Jesus, help me realize that you are always with me on my sometimes difficult journey through life, each and every day. Amen.

SEVENTH DAY

MORNING MEDITATION

The passion

Read Luke 22:14—23:56

At the last supper Jesus foretold his death when he took a loaf of bread, broke it, gave thanks, and said: "This is my body, which is given for you." Again he did the same when he took the cup and said: "This cup that is poured out for you is the new covenant in my blood." He added: "The Son of Man is going as it has been determined."

In Luke's gospel the passion of Jesus is not unexpected. His condemnation was understandable and, in a way, even unavoidable. The rulers and participants in the old, bedeviled order were not going to accept the kingdom of God that Jesus introduced into their world. This is something that has remained true in our world. Those who witness to the new, such as Archbishop Oscar Romero or Martin Luther King, Jr., not only knew that their work put their lives at risk but also foresaw that they would be killed.

Jesus had been living under this threat from the very beginning of his ministry. His own people had tried to kill him in Nazareth. The leaders of his world had been plotting to finish him off since he first appeared in public. His forerunner, John the Baptizer, had already been murdered.

Violence reigned all around Jesus. Yet he was going to overcome the violence of our world by his nonviolent response. He would let it rage and do whatever it could. He knew that violence would kill him, but he also knew that he would overcome it and rise again. He would ultimately triumph over violence and death.

Jesus and the apostles did not leave the table that night without a last discussion on who was the greatest among them. He told them he had come for no other reason but to serve, and to follow his example. He warned Peter that he would betray him, but that he had prayed for him. Peter would repent, and be called to render the service of strengthening the others. Then off they went, into the night.

It was Jesus's custom to go to the Mount of Olives to pray. While his disciples fell asleep he prayed, asking his Father to find another way for him, adding, "Not my will be done, but yours be done." An angel came to strengthen Jesus, as fear gripped him in the realization of what was to occur. Luke, the physician, describes that fear in an almost clinical way: "his sweat became like great drops of blood."

Suddenly, Judas arrived with a crowd. As Jesus was being arrested one of his disciples drew a sword and cut off the right ear of a slave of the high priest. Jesus touched the ear and healed it before he handed himself over. Then he was led to the high priest's house, and eventually, to his death on the cross.

Each of the evangelists have their own interpretation of what happened that night and the following day. Mark and Matthew wrote that Jesus said he gave his life as a "ransom," a price to be paid to the Father to free us from sin (Mk 10:45; Mt 20:28). John compares Jesus to the Lamb, to be sacrificed because of our sins (1:29, 36). As a non-Jew writing for a Gentile audience, Luke does not use those terms. His readers would not have understood them, just like many of us nowadays may have difficulties understanding them.

In Luke's gospel, it is one of the two criminals crucified with Jesus who offers Luke's understanding of Jesus' death. While Jesus is dying on the cross, the crowd and the soldiers shout at him, mockingly: "He saved others; let him save himself if he is the Messiah of God, his chosen one!" It sounded like an echo of the devil when he tempted Jesus in the desert.

One of the murderers joins their chorus, and he too shouts at Jesus: "Are you not the Messiah? Save yourself and us!" The other criminal, often called the good criminal, stops him, saying: "Do you not fear God, since you are under the same sentence of condemnation? And we indeed have been condemned justly, for we are getting what we deserve for our deeds, but this man has done nothing wrong." In the presence of Jesus, something had started to stir in this man's heart. At that moment, he knew that not only was Jesus counted among the lawless because of his goodness, but also that he and his goodness would triumph.

Turning to Jesus he asks to be with him in his kingdom. He is a bit vague about the timing, saying, "Jesus remember me, when you come into your kingdom." But Jesus is not at all vague in his response: "Truly, I tell you, today you will be with me in paradise." The victory had been won, evil overcome, and God's kingdom and rule restored. It was no longer a future hope but a present reality.

There is another person who sees through the misery of the moment: the commanding Roman officer. Luke mentions how he gave praise to God, saying, "Certainly this man was innocent." Even the crowds must have felt this, because they went home "beating their breasts."

FOR REFLECTION

- What are the conflicts that Jesus met when living the reign of God? Are there similar conflicts in your life?

- What does the good criminal's repentant appeal tell you? Does it in any way suggest the appeal you might make to Jesus?

- After Jesus' death and resurrection the reign of God was no longer a future hope, but a present option. What does this reality mean to you?

MORNING PRAYER

Lord Jesus, you have given your life for us.
Help me to respond with my whole life. Amen.

FAITH RESPONSE FOR TODAY

Visit a church and pray the way of the cross. Or if that is impossible, pray psalm 22.

EVENING MEDITATION

On the road to Emmaus

Read Luke 24:13–53

It was late in the afternoon when Cleopas and his companion left Jerusalem on their way to Emmaus. (Luke does not mention the name of the companion. Could it have been Cleopas' wife?) They were talking with each other about all that had happened in recent days.

From the story we can assume that they had gone to Jerusalem for the Passover celebrations, and having heard that Jesus was going to be there they were full of the hope "that he was the one to redeem Israel." But returning home from Jerusalem they felt disappointed, frustrated, and sad. They knew that some women had seen Jesus' empty tomb, and even that some angels had told the women Jesus was still alive. But like the apostles, Cleopas and his companion considered that story a bit of nonsense (24:11).

As Jesus caught up to them, he asked what they were talking about and why they looked so upset. They stopped on the road to tell him. Had he not heard what had happened to Jesus? How so many people had hoped that he was the Messiah, yet he had been arrested, condemned by the Jewish leaders, and executed by the Romans? They told him the story about the empty tomb and the angels seen there, adding that Jesus himself had not been seen.

Jesus reproaches them, saying, "Oh, how foolish you are!" and explains that they should see all that has happened in light of what the prophets had foretold. Jesus' words apply to us as well; we too should see him in light of the promises made of old. It is what his mother Mary did when she sang her Magnificat upon meeting Elizabeth, and it is what Zechariah did in his song at the birth of his son, John the Baptizer.

When they arrived at Cleopas' house in Emmaus, Jesus continued to walk on. But Cleopas and his companion invited him to stay. It was getting dark, and as the world had not yet been changed it remained dangerous to walk in that darkness.

Jesus stayed, but sitting at their table he changed his role. He was no longer the guest but the host as he took their bread, broke it, and gave it to them. He celebrated with them as he had with the disciples at their last supper together. At this they suddenly realized in whose presence they were.

According to Luke, Jesus then "vanished from their sight." This implies that Jesus did not leave them but was no longer visible. Jesus stayed with them as he had promised his apostles he would at the last supper, not visible but truly there. He left them with their bread, which Jesus had made his own. At the same time he left them with a way to recognize him, as well as a way to make themselves recognizable as his disciples as they in turn broke the bread.

Notwithstanding the darkness of night, Cleopas and his companion then "got up and returned to Jerusalem." Before they did that, they said to one another, "Were our hearts not burning within us, while he was talking to us?" They had felt what the apostles, the disciples, both women and men, and the good criminal had experienced in the presence of Jesus. A fire, a spirit that had been hidden in them had been enkindled and enlivened. It was as John the Baptizer had foretold: Jesus would baptize with fire and the Holy Spirit.

Arriving in Jerusalem, the two told their story to the eleven and the other disciples. They in turn told them that Jesus had appeared to Simon Peter, and that he was risen, indeed. Then, as an *apotheosis* or climax in the story, Jesus himself suddenly stands in their midst. He tells them, "Peace be with you!" and adds, "It is I, myself." Seeing their fear, Jesus assures them that he is not a ghost: "Touch me and see!" Then he showed them his hands and his feet. Touching him, they touched God, as we do when we receive the Eucharist on our tongue or in our hands.

Jesus then asked them for something to eat. They gave him a piece of broiled fish, which he ate with them. He then gave them, for the last time, an after-meal talk as he was accustomed to do. First he explained to them what he had been telling the two on the way to Emmaus, about his life being the fulfillment of what the prophets had foretold.

He then gave them their mission: "that repentance and forgiveness of sins is to be proclaimed in my name to all nations, beginning from Jerusalem." The old would be over and the reign of God re-introduced.

To enable them to do this, Jesus promised the disciples that they would be "clothed with power from on high," baptized, filled, dressed, equipped, and empowered with the Holy Spirit. Jesus then led them to Bethany, and blessing them, he was taken up to heaven.

The disciples returned to Jerusalem "with great joy," the joy Luke mentions numerous times in his gospel, from the very beginning to the end.

FOR REFLECTION

- Jesus sent his disciples, the ones he called his friends (12:4), out into the world with a mission to introduce the reign of God. This mission has been called by recent popes, the "civilization of love." How does this mission influence the life you live as one of Jesus' friends?

- How does the celebration of the Eucharist affect your awareness of the presence of Jesus in your life? Attend one weekday Mass this week. While there, make a conscious effort to connect what you celebrate during the Eucharist with your everyday life.

- How have your meditations on Luke's gospel influenced your thoughts, feelings, and actions during this retreat?

PRAYER SUGGESTION

Thank you, Lord Jesus, for the gospel of your disciple Luke. Thank you for your words which he recalled; they are an inspiration for me. Help me to respond to them in the Spirit you sent to us from the Father. Amen.

CONCLUSION

"Your kingdom come"

Read Luke 11:2

When he wrote his gospel, Luke knew that "many have undertaken to set down an orderly account of the events that have been fulfilled among us" (1:1). So why did he feel the need to write his own account of the good news? Did he want to complete the other gospels, thinking they had forgotten or overlooked certain important issues? Might he have wanted even to correct them? These are difficult questions to answer; but it is not difficult to notice what makes Luke's gospel different from the others.

Luke writes as a physician. Even if he was not a doctor (and we do not know for sure), he writes like one. He saw Jesus as a physician who came to heal, or to use a more literal translation of the word Luke uses for this process, he came to "save," to restore to health. Luke is interested in Jesus as the healer he describes, but he is also interested in the "patients" who were healed in Jesus' presence.

Luke was amazed by what had happened to these patients. Jesus brought them to new life. They began to sing and praise God, and act as they never had before. They lived a life in common with others who followed Jesus, loving God, their community, and the whole world. They were filled with joy in a way that Luke had never witnessed before in the grim world in which he lived.

Without a doubt, Luke's gospel is the happiest, the most joyful of the four. This joy began with Jesus' mother Mary, who, once aware of her pregnancy, sang:

My soul magnifies the Lord, and my spirit rejoices in God my Savior (1:46–47).

The healing power the disciples had experienced in Jesus' presence was shared by them, not only personally and individually but together with the communities they formed.

In his gospel, Luke refers thirty-eight times to the '"kingdom of God" Jesus came to introduce in our world. His gospel could be seen as one enormous prayer of invitation: "Father, hallowed be your name. Your kingdom come!" (11:2).

Luke never mentions the word "church" in his gospel. But his approach is very different in his second book, the Acts of the Apostles. Here the term "kingdom of God" is mentioned only six times. The emphasis in Acts is on "church," the communities of those living under the influence of God's Spirit, with the Spirit of Jesus (Acts 16:7) active in them. In Acts, the word "church" is mentioned nineteen times. It is here in these bread-breaking communities that the kingdom had come, is coming, and will come.

Being baptized, healed, and empowered with God's Spirit did not *only* mean that Christians were converted or reborn, or that they considered Jesus to be their healer, savior, and life-giver. It did not *only* mean that living under God's rule of love entailed striving after personal sanctification and holiness. Having been reborn and sanctified by the experience of God's healing and saving power, we are *also* called to mission in this world, just like Mary, the apostles, the seventy, and all who experienced God's Spirit.

"Clothed with power from on high," Christians follow the example of Jesus, sharing humanity's suffering and helping to serve its needs, as well as being spiritually and socially relevant to individuals, to society, and to the whole of creation.

Luke wanted to make it clear that Jesus Christ and all he stood for reaches beyond sermons and Scriptures. Christ calls us to live out his mission of peace, justice, and the integrity of creation as we further the reign of God, the "civilization of love."

This is what Luke wanted to clarify to Theophilus, for whom he wrote his book. The name "Theophilus" means both "lover of God" and "loved by God." It is a name that stands for you and me, and for all those of good will.

MY JOURNAL

MY JOURNAL

_____

_____

_____

_____

_____

_____

_____

_____

_____

_____

_____

_____

_____

_____

_____

_____

_____

_____

MY JOURNAL

_____

_____

_____

_____

_____

_____

_____

_____

_____

_____

_____

_____

_____

_____

_____

_____

_____

_____

_____

_____

MY JOURNAL

_____

_____

_____

_____

_____

_____

_____

_____

_____

_____

_____

_____

_____

_____

_____

_____

_____

_____

_____

MY JOURNAL

_____

_____

_____

_____

_____

_____

_____

_____

_____

_____

_____

_____

_____

_____

_____

_____

_____

_____

MY JOURNAL

MY JOURNAL

_____

_____

_____

_____

_____

_____

_____

_____

_____

_____

_____

_____

_____

_____

_____

_____

_____

_____

_____

_____

_____

MY JOURNAL
